Didn't our hearts burn within us as
he talked with us on the road?

- Luke 24:32 (NLT)

HOLIDAY ROAD

A Christmas Devotional

By Jason Byerly

FLANIGAN
PRESS

Cover art adapted from a vector by rudenok-angel/shutterstock.
Artwork on journal page and chapter pages by hoverfly/shutterstock.
Artwork on bonus section page by vecteezy.com.

First Printing, 2016
The author owns all rights to the devotions in this book but wishes to acknowledge that some of the work is adapted from the author's columns that previously appeared in *Southern Indiana Living Magazine*, *The Clarion News* and in the ebook *The Life Less Traveled*, 2011.

Flanigan Press

ISBN: 978-0692797624 (paperback)

www.jasonbyerly.com

For my girls.

You make every season
merry and bright.

CONTENTS

BONUS SECTION: Holidays throughout the Year

INTRODUCTION

Over two-thousand years ago a group of wise men took the first Christmas road trip. It sounds crazy to me because everyone knows the holidays are a terrible time to travel, but these guys were determined. They had a birthday party they just couldn't miss.

The Bible tells us, "When Jesus was born, some wise men from the east came to Jerusalem" (Matthew 2:1 NCV).

We don't know much about these guys for sure, except for the fact that they went through a lot of trouble to get to Jesus. They may have traveled for as long as two whole years.

Imagine that. A two-year road trip. Two years of traveling, waiting, watching and wondering if they were ever going to make it. Two years of asking the question, "Are we there yet?"

You know how road trips go. I'm sure there were plenty of pit stops and detours and maybe even a camel with a flat hoof or two. But, like I said, you just couldn't stop these guys. One way or another they were going to find Jesus.

Fortunately they had a little help. God provided them with a star to lead the way. Near as I can tell it was like Siri without all the talking.

I don't know about you, but I could use that same kind of help today. In the midst of the busyness of the Christmas season it can be tough to find Jesus.

The good news is that God is still in the business of guiding those who seek Him. He might not give us a special star this Christmas, but He does surround us with everyday reminders that point us back to Him.

Think of them as mile markers on the holiday road. You won't find them on the interstates or expressways, but only on the back roads to Bethlehem.

Over the following pages let's slow down and take the scenic route to Christmas. Let's chase after Jesus with the same determination as the wise men of old. After all, this is one birthday party we don't want to miss.

So what are you waiting for? It's time to begin our journey down the holiday road.

1

COOKIE CUTTER CHRISTMAS

Taste and see that the Lord is good.

– PSALM 34:8 (NLT)

Every Christmas my family makes cutout sugar cookies with all the holiday shapes. Stars, bells, angels, wreathes. You name it. We bake it. But this is no undertaking for sissies or Food Network wannabes. It's a massive yuletide baking blitz.

With two kids involved, the whole process is a huge production, and we set aside an entire day to crank these babies out for family and friends. To make it even more complicated, someone gave us a box of 101 plastic cookie cutters filled with shapes from every holiday you can imagine: shamrocks, pumpkins, eggs and even a football and helmet to celebrate the big game. Good luck finding a Christmas tree in that haystack.

When my oldest daughter was five, I stuck her with the job of digging out the ones we needed. I had a million things to do to get the assembly line rolling and figured she could handle the grunt work while I prepped the kitchen.

"Just find the Christmas shapes," I told her. I came back ten minutes later expecting to see Santa and reindeer. Instead, she had pulled out only two cookie cutters: a heart and a cross.

"Those are Christmas. Right, Dad?"

I stopped dead in my tracks, floored by the truth of what she had said. It was a holy moment.

"Yeah," I said, "they sure are."

It's easy to forget in the middle of the craziness of the holiday season that it all really comes down to that. A heart and a cross. "For this is how God loved the world: He gave his one and only Son, so that everyone who believes in him will not perish but have eternal life" (John 3:16 NLT).

After all the gifts are unwrapped, all the food eaten, all the stress and tension of the season released, be assured that when your head hits the pillow Christmas night, you are loved more than you know.

God's heart still beats for you. The cross is still the best gift of all time. And the friendship God offers is sweeter than any treat out of the oven.

Journal Prompts
for a Silent Night

What are the biggest distractions you face during the holiday season?

Read Luke 2:1-7. What does the birth of Jesus mean to you?

Draw a heart and a cross on an index card or small piece of paper and put it somewhere you'll see it every day to remind you what the Christmas season is all about.

God, thanks for your love for me. Thanks for your sacrifice on the cross. Help me to remember that this is what I'm celebrating at Christmas and all year long.

Amen

2

BIGGEST CHRISTMAS EVER!

But he gave up his place with God and made himself nothing.
He was born as a man and became like a servant.

- PHILIPPIANS 2:7 (NCV)

When I took out my trash tonight, I realized I needed more Christmas lights on my house. Our neighbors have more lights, but they have nice flat rooflines. Mine go straight up to a peak like a medieval cathedral. Our house is tiny. It's just all roof.

I have to do my human fly routine just to get anything on the front of the house. I'd sworn it off this year, but now? Now, I'm not so sure.

See, I have this problem, this compulsion, you might say. It's an unreasonable drive to try and top myself every Christmas—with my lights, with my presents, with everything. Each year I want to have the biggest and best Christmas ever. For some people, the movie *National Lampoon's Christmas Vacation* is a comedy. For me, it's a documentary.

But I'm not alone in my obsession. I did some research the other day to find some like-minded Christmas enthusiasts.

Did you know that the world record for the most lights strung on an artificial Christmas tree stands at 518,838?[1] I'm not even close to that. In fact, my tree looks like Charlie Brown's compared to the 115-foot fir tree that just went up this year at the Citadel Outlets in Los Angeles. It claims to be the tallest live-cut tree in the world.[2]

And our Christmas stockings? Don't even get me started. A group in North Carolina last year made one that's 139 feet long and 74 feet wide.[3] That thing can hold a serious amount of candy.

Oh, and how about snowmen? How can I hope to compete with the industrious townsfolk of Bethel, Maine, who built a 122-foot tall snow woman back in 2008?[4] She had trees for arms, for crying out loud. Trees!

Okay, so maybe you don't have to have the tallest tree or the most lights or the largest snowman to have the biggest and best Christmas ever. Maybe Christmas isn't about the biggest and the best at all. Maybe it's actually about smallness, the smallness of a great, big God who made Himself tiny enough to fit in a manger.

So, in that light, I guess I need to reevaluate what it means to have the biggest Christmas ever. Maybe, instead of topping last year's decorations and presents, I need to top myself in other ways.

What if I focused on bigger faith, bigger hope and bigger love? What if I had bigger grace to offer the difficult people around me and bigger humility to admit when I'm the difficult person in their lives? Or how about bigger courage to do the crazy, risky things I know God's called me to do?

Maybe it all comes down to trusting a bigger God who loved me enough to get little. World record material? Maybe not. Best Christmas ever? Absolutely.

Have you ever overdone it at Christmas? Ever fallen into the bigger-is-better mentality?

Read Philippians 2:5-9. How did Jesus make Himself small that first Christmas? What did He have to give up to do it?

What needs to get bigger in your heart to make this the best Christmas ever? Faith? Hope? Love? Courage? Humility?

*God, thank you for making yourself small
enough to enter into my world. Help me to
have big faith in you today.*

Amen

3

NOT A CREATURE WAS STIRRING

Be still, and know that I am God.

– PSALM 46:10 (NIV)

The man who wrote *'Twas the Night Before Christmas* obviously never met my kids. Remember that line about children being nestled all snug in their beds?[5] That is not happening in my house. Not a creature was stirring? Please. The last thing my kids want to do on Christmas Eve is sleep.

A few years ago, we had the worst battle ever. My youngest daughter was five, and she was so hyped up over opening presents that she just would not go down. I'd already put her to bed, but she kept getting up, and refused to even get under the covers and relax.

Unfortunately, it was one of those Christmases when we had something big to set up, which meant I needed to see some serious nestling in a hurry. However, she would have none of it.

So, I did the only thing I knew to do. I played the Santa card.

Me: "Honey, if you don't go to sleep, Santa can't come."
Strong-Willed Daughter: "But Daddy!"

9

Me: "Look, if we're awake, we won't get any presents."
Strong-Willed Daughter: "But Daddy!"
Me: "If I'm still in your room, Santa's not going to stop."
Strong-Willed Daughter: "But Daddy!"
Me: "Santa will be here any minute!"
Strong-Willed Daughter: "BUT DADDY!"

As you can see, it worked really well. The harder I tried to get her to sleep, the more she was convinced she had to stay up. Her emotions were escalating, and she was about to go nuclear on me.

Thankfully, that's when we heard the crash.

My wife had crept out to fill the stockings and dropped something hard on the marble around our fireplace.

The second my daughter heard it, everything changed. Without a word, she dove into bed, squeezed her eyes shut and started waving me away with her hand. Her message was clear. Get out of my room. Do not blow this for me.

We didn't hear another peep out of her the rest of the night.

It's funny how kids hate to stop, isn't it? But when it comes to the holiday season, they might just be learning from our example. Christmas often feels more like a race than a time of rest. We cram the season with shopping, wrapping, baking, decorating, attending programs, parties and family gatherings, and we wonder why emotions run high over the holidays. We wonder why we feel stressed. We wonder why it doesn't feel like Christmas.

It's not exactly a season of peace on Earth.

The truth is if we want to experience peace, we have to control our pace. At Christmas, and every other day, God longs for us to stop and release the responsibility of running the universe to Him. The pressure's off. We can't do everything, be everywhere and solve the problems of the world. That's His job.

I wanted my daughter to sleep so I could give her a gift, and in the same way God is waiting for us to stop so that He can give us what we truly need. God wants us to rest so we can be blessed.

Like any good father at Christmas, God is excited about giving to His children. Our job is simply to stop and receive.

Journal Prompts for a Silent Night

Would you say this Christmas feels more holy or hectic? If it's hectic, what's making it hard to stop and rest?

Read Luke 10:38-42. Which sister in the story sounds more like you?

Set aside ten minutes a day to just stop and be still before God. Ask Him to quiet your soul and refocus your heart on Him.

God, thank you for the gift of rest. Show me how to create space in my life to be refreshed and renewed. Please help me to stop today and spend time enjoying you.

Amen

4

THE WAITING GAME

But as for me, I watch in hope for the Lord.
I wait for God my Savior; my God will hear me.

– MICAH 7:7 (NIV)

I'm standing in line at Toys "R" Us as I write this. Trust me, I've got the time. It's the Saturday before Thanksgiving, and every person in central Kentucky is in line in front of me. My wife is doing the math and telling me how I messed up and picked the wrong line. Every line, of course, is moving faster than ours.

Yes, Christmas is a waiting game. Waiting in shopping lines. Waiting in traffic. Waiting for cookies to bake. Waiting for holiday movies to come on TV. Waiting for vacation. Waiting for packages. Waiting for cards. Waiting to see Santa. Waiting for snow. Waiting to put up the tree. Waiting for family to arrive. Waiting for family to leave. Waiting to unwrap presents.

Waiting. Waiting. Waiting. We're all waiting for something this Christmas.

If you think all this Christmas waiting is hard, just think of how long God restrained Himself by waiting. From the time before time began, He waited and waited and waited, until the perfect moment arrived, a mysterious point in history, when He would take on flesh, step into our world and restore the broken relationship with His creation.

For centuries before that first Christmas, all of Israel had been waiting too. There'd been rumors, of course. Prophets had spoken of a Messiah. He'd be born in Bethlehem, they said. Born of a virgin, even. And He would come to set the world free. So the people held this hope close their hearts and waited some more.

One day an angel appeared to young girl named Mary. Then her waiting began.

Imagine nine of months of waiting, waiting to tell your fiancée that you're pregnant, and by the way, it's God's child. Imagine waiting for Joseph's response, waiting for him to say something, anything, but instead he just walks away. More waiting for Mary, waiting—hoping—for God to bring Joseph back.

Imagine waiting as your Creator grew inside of you: embryo, fetus, infant, God. Imagine waiting for the impossible to happen, for the One they call Almighty, to be born into the world through you.

As it was with Mary, so it is with us. Christ is formed inside of us in the waiting, but only if we wait with purpose.

This Christmas we'll all do our fair share of waiting, but how we wait, that's up to us. Will we grit our teeth with an impatient let's-get-this-over-with kind of waiting or will we lean into it, enjoying the anticipation of God breaking into our world once again?

What are you waiting for this Christmas?

How can waiting help you to grow closer to God?

What does it look like to wait on purpose?

God, you are worth the wait. Help me not to be
impatient this Christmas but to learn to use all
the waiting as a chance to focus on you.

Amen

5

CATALOG OF DREAMS

All of my longings lie open before you, Lord;
my sighing is not hidden from you.

- PSALM 38:9 (NIV)

When I was a kid, the world didn't get serious about Christmas until Thanksgiving had passed. For me, though, it began the day the Service Merchandise catalog arrived.

The second I got my hands on it, I blew past the clothes and luggage and went straight for the magic tucked away in the back. Atari cartridges. Star Wars action figures. G. I. Joes. These carefully staged photographs popped from the pages, promising to sweep me up into a world of adventure.

This was the stuff dreams were made of and Christmas lists. Very long Christmas lists. After the list came the waiting, the yearning, the hours that stretched into days, weeks and months. It was the season when time stood still.

Then, just when the waiting became unbearable, Christmas arrived. Mysteries wrapped in bright paper appeared under our tree. And finally, the moment came, the awesome moment when I hooked my fingers into the sharply creased folds on the top of the first present and ripped the paper away.

In that moment the hope and magic that I had once only experienced in the pages of a catalog came to life. My dreams now had dimension and weight. I could touch them, hold them and play with them at last. What once seemed a world away had now come into my world.

That's the true magic of Christmas, the gift of the infant God born in a Bethlehem stable. What once seemed a world away has now come into our world. Jesus, called the Word of God, "became flesh and blood and moved into the neighborhood" (John 1:14 MSG).

God was no longer distant. He was no longer unreachable. He was one of us. We could touch Him, hold Him and be with Him at last.

Long before children made lists for St. Nick, our desires were an open book to God. As the poet David once prayed, "All of my longings lie open before you, Lord; my sighing is not hidden from you" (Psalm 38:9 NIV).

The prophets of Israel even began a list, a catalog of sorts, that told of the promised One who would come as the answer to the deepest wishes of the human heart, wishes of belonging, healing and love. Jesus came to bring the good gifts of the God's kingdom to life.

God knows the desire of your heart. He knows the most painful longing in your soul. He knows your secret hurts, your fears and the ache that can only be filled by His presence. 2,000 years ago, Jesus came to earth to fulfill that longing, and He's still in the same business today.

Journal Prompts
for a Silent Night

What were some of the things on your childhood Christmas list?

What are you longing for this Christmas? What heavenly gifts, such as peace, healing, forgiveness or love are on your wish list today?

Do you trust God with the desires of your heart? What makes that challenging or easy for you?

God, you know me inside and out. You know my
heart, my hopes and my dreams. Thank you for the
gift of Jesus who meets my deepest needs.

Amen

6

No Room in the Inn

Then Christ will make his home
in your hearts as you trust in him.

- Ephesians 3:17 (NLT)

The problem wasn't that there was no room in the inn. The problem was there was no room in any inn, anywhere. You see the entire Gulf Coast was under a mandatory evacuation, and I was running from a hurricane with a pregnant wife.

Sure, I know what you're thinking. Most people don't go to the beach during a hurricane, but I'm from Indiana. What do I know? To be fair, most of the week they were just calling it a tropical storm. When they'd finally upgraded it to a hurricane, it was still three days away from making landfall. That would give us a good couple of days at the beach, right?

The best part was that we had the place to ourselves. Beaches are surprisingly vacant during an impending natural disaster. However, we only got to enjoy one afternoon in the sand before the official word came down. The state had ordered everyone evacuated by 6:00 a.m. the next morning.

We thought we'd get a jump on traffic and leave at dinner, but everyone else had the same idea. And when I say everyone, I mean everyone in the entire Florida panhandle.

We sat in gridlock that would put Congress to shame. Then we waited some more. By one in the morning, were still trying to get across the state line.

I started calling hotels, but of course, all of them were full. I thought the farther away we got from the beach, the better our chances, but a wave of refugees had a head start on us, filling every possible bed between the ocean and the Great Lakes—every bed except for one.

I finally managed to score us a room at a decrepit roadside inn on a back road in Alabama. Fortunately the drug dealers and escaped convicts who usually stayed there were evacuating too, so they had plenty of room. But, then again, so did the Bates Motel.

When I opened the door to our room, my wife took one look inside and said, "I am not sleeping in there." She was ready to take her chances with the hurricane.

Hmm, pregnant wife, long journey, no place to stay. It was beginning to sound a lot like Christmas. I don't how Mary reacted when Joseph told her they would be sleeping in a barn, but I'm sure it didn't exactly seem like an accommodation fit for a king. Of course, Jesus was no ordinary king.

He was born in humility and poverty because He wanted to reach the spiritually humble and the poor, people who were desperate enough to make room in their hearts for Him.

The same is still true this Christmas. My calendar is packed. My shopping list is full. But my heart? I'm praying that I will make plenty of room there for the King who came to set me free.

No room in the inn is one thing, but no room in me? Not this Christmas.

Journal Prompts
for a Silent Night

If your heart were a home, would Jesus feel welcome there today? Is there room for Him? If not, what's getting in the way?

Imagine Jesus was walking through the rooms of your heart right now. What are some of the things He would see in there that would make Him smile?

Is there anything in your heart Jesus would want to get rid of? Any old regrets, self-loathing or pride? Any lies you're believing about yourself that He would want to pitch to the curb?

God, you are welcome in my heart today. Make yourself at home. I invite you to live in me and through me right now.

Amen

7

THE BRIGHTEST BULB
ON THE TREE

"I am the light of the world.
Whoever follows me will never walk in darkness,
but will have the light of life."

– JOHN 8:12 (NIV)

We bought a pre-lit Christmas tree to protect our sanity. With a newborn and three-year-old in the house, we were lucky to keep everyone fed and bathed, let alone string lights on a tree. We thought it would make things easier.

Turns out, though, what we really needed was a post-lit tree, one where the store sends a guy to your house to replace the lights after the junky ones start burning out. Since I haven't found anyone willing to do that yet, it falls on me.

Every November I burrow into the web of wires and branches tracking down bad lights. Over the years we've added so many new lights that it's almost impossible figure out where each dark strand begins or ends.

A couple of hours into the process I usually just lose it and start yanking wires. I was making great progress this year when my wife pointed out that I had removed several strands that were working.

Sometimes my life, like my tree, feels like a tangled mess. Complicated relationships, fears and problems short circuit my joy and darken my vision. Like the lights on my pre-lit tree, some areas of life just don't work like they should.

It's all such a jumble that I could never fix it on my own. The solution, however, isn't to replace a broken bulb or two. What I really need is to start from scratch. I need a whole a new tree.

2 Corinthians 5:17 says, "This means that anyone who belongs to Christ has become a new person. The old life is gone; a new life has begun" (NLT).

Jesus didn't show up in Bethlehem to make our lives just a little bit better, to replace a bulb here and there. He came to give us an entirely new kind of life, a life that is lit by a hope that never dims.

I may not be the brightest bulb on the tree, but I do know this. Jesus is the light of the world. As I turn to Him this Christmas season, I begin to see even the darkest situations in my life in a whole new light.

Journal Prompts
for a Silent Night

The Bible says that Jesus is the Light of the World. What does that mean to you today?

Reflect on your history with God. What tangled messes has God helped you navigate in the past?

Are there any complicated situations you're facing right now? How can Jesus bring new light and hope to this problem?

God, thank you for sending Jesus to be the light of my world. Please show me how to untangle the messes of life and take your hope into the darkness.

Amen

8

SHOPPING MACHINE

For the Son of Man came to seek and save those who are lost.

– LUKE 19:10 (NLT)

Christmas shopping with my wife scares me. She is a kind and gentle woman eleven months out of the year. December, however, is another matter entirely.

During the Christmas season something frightening occurs. She flips an internal switch and becomes a laser-focused shopping machine bent on finding the perfect gifts. She is relentless. Tireless. Unstoppable. There is no way I can even begin to keep up.

For example, the other day we were walking into Target having a casual conversation when her inner shopping machine came on-line. I could almost hear the circuitry is her head buzzing to life. "Uh oh," I thought. I'd seen this happen before. The second we stepped into the store, it was game on.

The next thing I knew I was being dragged through the aisles like a fallen water-skier. There would be no stopping, no browsing and certainly no bathroom breaks. The Tannenbaum Terminator would not be delayed. By the time we got to the dolls, I was ready to collapse into a sobbing heap on the floor.

But my wife was just getting started.

She dropped me like a bad habit at the Barbie aisle and went straight for a holiday doll. Was that an infrared sensor I saw gleaming in her eye? The last thing I remember was hearing the words, "I'll . . . be . . . baack" before she marched off in search of the next item on her list.

Okay, so maybe I made the part up about the infrared sensor, and maybe my wife doesn't talk like Schwarzenegger. But her single-minded focus on finding gifts is no exaggeration. I have to hand it to her, though. At the end of it all, she always finds incredible gifts at unbelievable prices for the people she loves.

Isn't that just like Christmas? An incredible gift at an unbelievable price for those who are loved.

I don't know where you are spiritually this Christmas, but I can tell you there was a time in my life that I was far from God. What I didn't understand, though, was that God was never far from me.

You see, I was on God's wish list—we all are—and God was laser-focused in His pursuit of me. Not in a pushy, domineering way, but just patiently persistent, inviting and offering Himself to me over and over again.

He was tireless. His love interminable. I couldn't outrun Him, outsin Him or outlast Him. I soon understood why poet Francis Thompson called God the "Hound of Heaven."[6]

If Christmas is about anything, it's about God's tenacious pursuit of each one of us. Because we could never reach God on our own, He came to earth to reach out to us.

At Christmas we remember that God is still with us today, pursuing, wooing, and never giving up on His relationship with us. Even if you don't believe in God, He will never stop believing in you.

Have you ever been determined to buy a specific gift for someone that was hard to find? Why didn't you give up?

Have you ever felt like God had given up on you? Have you ever given up on God? What were the circumstances?

Read Luke 15:3-6. How does it make you feel to realize that God relentlessly pursues you? What would it look like if you pursued Him with the same focus?

God, you are the Hound of Heaven. Thank you for pursuing me with a love that just won't quit. Please help me to chase after you with all of my heart today.

Amen

9

DECK THE HALLS

"And in him you too are being built together to become
a dwelling in which God lives by his Spirit."

– EPHESIANS 2:22 (NIV)

Two years ago my wife and I flipped a house for Christmas. We took a 30-year-old fixer-upper and completely renovated it inside and out. Fortunately it was only three feet tall.

It was the dollhouse my wife's grandfather had built for her when she was eight years old. The house had sat in our attic for the last several years waiting for the day our girls would be old enough to appreciate it. The Christmas they were six and nine, we decided it was finally time.

However, it wasn't going to be easy. Structurally the dollhouse was as solid as a brick. My wife's grandfather was an old-school carpenter and built things to last, but the years had not been kind. It was caked in the accumulated grime of almost three decades of storage. The colors had faded. The wallpaper had peeled away, and whatever furniture that had once inhabited it was long gone.

No doubt about it, this house was going to need some serious work. We knew, though, that the effort would be totally worth it.

33

The look on our girls' faces on Christmas morning would be priceless.

God feels the same way about each of us. We are all certainly fixer-uppers, works in progress on the path of spiritual transformation. We don't just need a fresh coat of paint. We need the fresh life of Christ in us.

As we walk with Jesus, we undergo what author Dallas Willard calls the renovation of the heart.[7] It is the painstaking process by which we are shaped into the likeness of God's Son. Day by day, hour by hour, God is restoring us to His original design.

A ton of work? You bet. But in God's eyes, it's totally worth it. He can't wait to see the look on your face when the renovation is finally complete.

The apostle Paul, who underwent a radical makeover himself, assures us, "God, who began the good work within you, will continue his work until it is finally finished on the day when Christ Jesus returns" (Philippians 1:6 NLT).

On that day, you will be like Jesus. Those old persistent habits you struggle with will be history. Your selfishness and pride will be no more. You will finally be everything you were meant to be from the beginning.

So, this Christmas don't be too hard on yourself. Don't lose patience when you are less than your best. You are under construction. Give yourself some grace. God certainly has, and this grace will continue its work in you until it is finished.

Journal Prompts
for a Silent Night

Have you ever renovated a house or worked on a home improvement project? What was frustrating and rewarding about the process?

Celebrate how far God has brought you. How are you different from the person you used to be?

Where are you still a work in progress? What's the next step in the renovation of your heart?

God, thank you that I am not the person I used to be.
Help me to cooperate with you as you renovate my heart
and show me what you want to change today.

Amen

10

SELF ON THE SHELF

Do nothing out of selfish ambition or vain conceit.
Rather, in humility value others above yourselves.

– PHILIPPIANS 2:3 (NIV)

Back in the seventies, we didn't have Elf On the Shelf dolls. We had the elf in the window. He would appear any time I started acting like a brat. I never actually saw him myself, but during the Christmas season, whenever I pouted or threw a fit, my parents would say, "Uh oh, I think I just saw an elf at the window. I hope he doesn't tell Santa you're acting like this."

It worked every time. After all, no kid wants to end up on the naughty list. Your entire Christmas is at stake.

In retrospect, this network of secret elf police seems a bit fascist to me. It sounds like East Berlin during the Cold War. Someone is watching your every move.

I grew up believing the same thing about God. He sees everything. He knows everything, and He doesn't even need elf informants to tell Him when I mess up.

Yet, what I've discovered is that God is for me, not against me. He's not waiting for me to blow it. He's waiting for me to come to

Him.

Thankfully God's not into the naughty and nice list, though He certainly has the right to be. Instead, He's into the forgiven list, and He wants to write your name on it.

Some days that can be hard to believe. God loves me for me? It sounds too good to be true, so we end up trying to earn it. Our whole lives become one big performance striving for the love of God and others. If we don't really believe we're loved by God, we'll go to people for that affirmation instead.

And the worst part? It puts all the focus on us. How am I doing? Are people mad at me? Are they pleased? Which list am I on today?

Maybe it's time to take ourselves off the list altogether. Let's take our cue from the apostle Paul who said, "It matters very little to me what you think of me, even less where I rank in popular opinion. I don't even rank myself" (1 Corinthians 4:3 MSG). Paul decided to leave the evaluating up to God, a God who corrects us when we need it, but loves us like a good Father nonetheless.

This Christmas, I say we ditch the naughty and nice list and put our elves away. Instead, let's start a new tradition called self on the shelf. When I'm tempted to beat myself up over the past, time to put myself on the shelf. When I'm obsessing over what someone else thinks of me, time to put myself on the shelf. When I'm easily offended by family and friends, it's definitely time to myself on the shelf.

During this holiday season, let's look for every opportunity to focus on loving God and the people He sends our way, not to make God love us, but because He already does.

*Journal Prompts
for a Silent Night*

Do you struggle with people pleasing or obsess over your past failures? What does this look like in your life?

Are you often irritated by others, easily offended or frustrated when people don't do things your way?

Practice self-forgetfulness today. When you're tempted with selfishness or worried about what others think of you, just say, "self on the shelf" and redirect your thoughts towards God and the needs of others.

God, there is no one more selfless than you. Show me how to be like that. Help me to forget myself today so that I'm free to enjoy life and serve others.

Amen

11

SING WE NOW OF CHRISTMAS

The Word became a human and lived among us.

– JOHN 1:14 NCV

Just because you heard it in a Christmas song doesn't necessarily mean it's true. Take *Santa Claus Is Coming to Town* for instance. It tells kids they had better be on their best behavior if they want Christmas presents. Seriously? I've known kids who practically burned their house to the ground and still found a mountain of toys under their tree.

And c'mon, nobody is buying the story that Grandma got run over by a reindeer. Where was Grandpa at the time of the incident? Did Grandma have any enemies? Who's the beneficiary of her life insurance policy? We've all seen enough crime drama to know this case warrants further investigation.

Of all the erroneous Christmas songs, however, none is more misleading than *Away In a Manger*. It's a sweet song. I'll give you that. In fact, I can go 95% of the way with it. There's just one part that flies in the face of all I know about parenthood:

The cattle are lowing,
The baby wakes,
But little Lord Jesus,
No crying He makes.[8]

No crying He makes? Any parents see a problem with this? I'm no baby expert, but I am a dad of two daughters who have taught me the value of a good night's sleep. Baby sleep is gold. And fragile. If a mooing cow had startled either of my kids from a nap, they would have screamed their heads off. Most normal babies would have done the same thing.

If Jesus was anything, He was normal. Yes, He was God in the flesh, but that flesh was real with no unfair advantages.

The Bible says that Jesus shared in our humanity and was "fully human in every way" (Hebrews 2:17 NIV). That includes crying. In fact, as an adult He wept over the death of a friend and over those who refused to turn to Him for help.

Jesus knew firsthand the pain of a broken heart. He knew tears, rejection and grief. He wasn't simply like us. He was one of us.

It's comforting to know that when it comes to my worst day, Jesus has already been there, done that. That's the dirty reality of Christmas that doesn't fit into a pretty holiday song—that God gets it, that He understands how hard it can be to be you.

But not only does He get it, He actually loved us enough to do something about it. For a night or two Jesus lived away in a manger, but that manger led to a cross and the cross to an empty tomb, and there our tears of pain can become tears of joy. Joy to the world. The Lord has come.

Now that truth I can buy. That truth gets me through the long, dark night. That truth is worth singing about at Christmas or any time of year.

Journal Prompts
for a Silent Night

What is your favorite Christmas carol? Why do you love it?

Is it easier for you to see Jesus as fully God or fully human? Why is the other one harder for you to embrace?

What is the hardest thing you've gone through this year? How does it make you feel to realize that Jesus knows exactly what you're going through?

God, thank you for sending me a Savior who entered into my heart-ache and pain. I'm so grateful you understand me, that you cry with me and give me joy to sustain me through the darkest times.

Amen

12

THE SHOW MUST GO ON

Imitate God, therefore, in everything you do,
because you are his dear children.

EPHESIANS 5:1 (NLT)

You never know when you're going to need an extra baby Jesus this time of year. Take the Christmas of 2008, for example. I needed five baby Jesuses, well, actually six, but who could have predicted the last one?

It was the biggest Christmas show of my life. My team got to take over the Christmas Eve services for our church, which was a huge deal. Five performances. 13,000 people. They even televised the thing a week later.

A smarter man would have used a doll for baby Jesus, but not me. I couldn't settle for anything less than a real, live baby. This was Jesus' birthday, for crying out loud, a gold, frankincense and myrrh kind of day. A cheap, plastic doll would never do.

Remember that old show business maxim, never work with kids or animals? Well, I threw that right out the window. Sure, infants are unpredictable. And yes, our actress who played Mary had never actually held a live baby before in her life. But as long as she

45

didn't drop the kid, what could possibly go wrong?

I knew if we found the right babies, we would be home free. So I went straight to the expert, our nursery director, to help me cast the show. "I need five professional babies," I told her. "Give me the good kind, the kind don't cry."

Sure enough, she rustled up five great babies, each apparently a budding actor in his or her own right. Rehearsals went without a hitch. Then we landed on opening night. The big moment had arrived. Twenty minutes into it the lights came up on baby Jesus #1. We all held our breath and then witnessed show business magic.

The baby was a pro. No crying. No stinky diapers. Nothing but cuteness. My live baby gamble had paid off, making me look like a genius, until, that is, we came to the second night.

I knew baby Jesus #2 was trouble the moment he arrived. I think I heard the kid yelling before he even got in the building. He was fussy, his mom said. Just hungry.

No problem, I thought. The show starts in an hour. Surely he'd calm down by then, right?

I waited out in the house, watching the room fill up. The ushers brought out extra chairs. Standing room only. I'd never seen the church that full.

Then, just before the service began, the director frantically ran out from backstage. "Baby Jesus is screaming his head off," he said. "We need a stand in!"

A stand in? We were only moments away from the Bethlehem stable scene. If we didn't move fast, Mary and Joseph would be sitting there empty-handed.

Fortunately, I happened to have an extra baby lying around that year. My newborn daughter was just six weeks old. Now all I had to do was find her in a dark auditorium packed with thousands of people. Where would I even start?

Then, in what I consider to be my own Christmas miracle, I spotted my wife in the back of the room. "Quick," I said, "Swaddle that kid!"

We sprinted down the hall to the backstage door, stripping off her girly PJs as we ran. Hopefully no one would notice the pink onesie. With only seconds to spare, we passed her over to the stagehand who delivered her right into Mary's arms seconds before the lights came up on Bethlehem.

Suffice it to say, my daughter stole the show. In my completely objective opinion she was the best baby Jesus since the original.

Now you may not be producing a church musical this season, but with all of your shopping, baking and family events, you may feel like you're staging a major production. You don't have to be on a stage to have plenty of Christmas drama in your life. You may even be facing some fussy characters who refuse to cooperate with your vision of a perfect Christmas.

But like my daughter you may also have an opportunity to stand in for Jesus. After all, He came into a broken world to reach out to the hurting and the lost. This Christmas, if we keep our eyes open, we may just get the chance to do the same.

Playing Santa is one thing, but playing Jesus? That's sure to make a Christmas you'll never forget.

Journal Prompts
for a Silent Night

Who are the people who have stood in for Jesus in your life? Who has loved you unconditionally, served you and spoken truth to help you grow?

What would it look like for you to play Jesus for others? What would need to change in your life to show more of Jesus to the world?

Where you can you stand in for Jesus today? Who needs your love, help or attention?

God, help me to share your love this Christmas season. Please show me how I can represent Jesus to those who need hope, help and forgiveness. I pray the drama of the holidays would never distract me from loving people in your name.

Amen

13

THE REAL ISLAND
OF MISFIT TOYS

God sets the lonely in families.

- PSALM 68:6 (NIV)

What was your favorite Christmas cartoon from childhood? Was it *Frosty the Snowman*? *A Charlie Brown Christmas*? *How the Grinch Stole Christmas*? All classics, for sure. In my opinion, though, it's tough to compete with *Rudolph the Red-Nosed Reindeer*, a holiday cartoon that stands the test of time.

Rudolph had it all: Santa, flying reindeer, elves, a snow monster and a Christmas blizzard that threatened the happiness of children around the globe. But the appeal of Rudolph for me isn't any of those things. It's the enduring theme of a band of misfits looking for a home.

In one season or another, we can all relate.

You ever been judged for your appearance? For Rudolph, of course, it was his nose. For you maybe it's your age, your clothes, or your accent.

If not your appearance, maybe you've been rejected for your passion. Remember Hermey, the elf who wanted to be dentist?

When we chase dreams that others don't understand, it can leave us isolated and misunderstood.

Or perhaps you're like the doll on the Island of Misfit Toys, cast aside for reasons that have never been clear. The Charlie-in-the-Box, the square-wheeled train and the other misfit toys had their obvious quirks, but the doll? No one knows why the doll was a misfit, and maybe you're asking the same questions about yourself.

What's wrong with me? Why don't I have the kind of friend-ships everyone else seems to have?

Even if you've had deep friendships in the past, you may find yourself in a season of loneliness today. And Christmas? Christmas, with its images of family, home and togetherness, can make our feelings of isolation all the worse.

But the good news is that God has a thing for the lonely. He sets them in families, the Scripture says. As for rejects, he turns them to royalty. And misfits? He's sends them on a mission to change the world.

Just ask the shepherds. Socially, these guys were the least of the last. Yet, God chose them to be the first to hear about the birth of His Son and share the story with all of Bethlehem. "After seeing him, the shepherds told everyone what had happened and what the angel had said to them about this child. All who heard the shepherds' story were astonished" (Luke 2:17-18 NLT).

God picked the shepherds, and God picks you. That's the message of Christmas. We are chosen. We are wanted. We are loved.

Jesus came to earth to invite us to a home where we truly belong. That place is called the kingdom of God. It's not an Island of Misfit Toys but a family where we find our perfect fit at last.

Have you ever felt like a misfit? Which character from *Rudolph the Red-Nosed Reindeer* can you relate to the most?

How does it make you feel to know that you are chosen and wanted by God? Have you experienced God's love and acceptance through other believers? If not, begin praying for God to connect you with Christians who will reflect the Father's love for you.

Who are the misfits in your life who need to know God has a place for them? How can you reach out to them today?

God, thank you that I always have a home with you and that I am never alone. Help me to reach out to those who are lonely or lost today.

Amen

14

UP ON THE ROOFTOP

So I recommend having fun.

– ECCLESIASTES 8:15 (NLT)

My senior year in college, Santa came just after midnight. I was living in a house with seven other guys, most of whom were nestled all snug in their beds when we heard the noise on the roof.

The prancing and pawing of hooves? It didn't seem likely. After all, we were a little old for reindeer games. However, it did sound like footsteps. Heavy footsteps. Living on campus had prepared us to expect the unexpected, but this was a new one. We'd had drunks on our doorstep but never anyone on our roof.

Of course, at Christmas these things tend to happen.

We raced downstairs ready for a fight, but by the time we reached the front door, the noise had stopped. Someone, however, had definitely been in the house. Inside the living room, beneath the branches of our shabby Christmas tree, sat eight brightly wrapped presents. "Hey, guys," I said, "They have our names on them. It wasn't a burglar. It was Santa!"

And that's when they knew they'd been had.

My roommate Steve and I had planned the whole thing. I had planted the gifts while he climbed the TV antenna to stomp on the roof. Once he started making racket, it was up to me to get everyone downstairs.

Steve and I didn't have much money, but we had plenty of creativity so we had gone to a dollar store and chosen a present specifically suited for each friend. As we distributed the gifts, the clock began to run backwards, and we all became like children again. The pressures of finals, job hunting and post-graduation plans melted away like a snowman on a hot afternoon.

Everyone tore into their packages with the wide-eyed wonder of kids on Christmas morning. The financial wizard got a package of play money. The future cop got a potato gun. And on and on down the line.

The Christmas spirit was so thick you could cut it with a knife. We played. We laughed. We became kids again, temporarily free of the expectations and responsibilities that come with grown-up life.

Jesus once said that unless we become like little children we will never enter the kingdom of heaven. He said God's kingdom belongs to kids and to those like them who are prepared to receive what God has to offer as a free gift (Matthew 18:2-4).

This Christmas don't take yourself, your to-do list and all of your worries too seriously. Kids don't. Jesus said to be like them. So lighten up. Relax and have some spontaneous fun.

Start a snowball fight. Surprise a friend with a toy. Risk your dignity as you create moments of silliness and laughter. Play Santa to someone in an unexpected way, and I guarantee that you'll find that the greatest surprise will be your own.

Journal Prompts
for a Silent Night

Do you think God is fun? Do you picture Him smiling or serious? Could God have created penguins, sunsets or puppies without smiling? Ask God to reveal His fun side to you today.

When was the last time you had fun? When have you laughed the hardest? Do something silly, spontaneous or playful this week.

Play dates aren't just for kids. Who do you know who needs some joy in their life? Grab them for a play date as soon as possible and make unforgettable memories together.

God, you are a God of surprises and fun. Thank you for the joy and laughter you bring my way. Help me to lighten up and not take myself so seriously this Christmas.

Amen

15

O CHRISTMAS TRAIN

Bear with each other and forgive one another if any of you
has a grievance against someone. Forgive as the Lord forgave you.

– COLOSSIANS 3:13 (NIV)

I used to have a cat named Tigger who hated our Christmas train. It was his mortal enemy. Sherlock Holmes had Moriarty. Batman had the Joker. Tigger had the GreatLand Holiday Express that circled our tree every Christmas.

I can't blame him. The train was huge and had the most realistic locomotive sounds I've ever heard on a toy. Its engine chug-a-chugged like a champ, and it had a whistle that made me think twice about crossing the tracks. To Tigger, I'm sure it looked like a big, noisy rat.

Whenever I ran the train, Tigger would stalk it. He'd crouch down beside the track, his hind legs bunched up and wiggling behind him, waiting for the opportunity to strike.

Once, when it came around the bend, he pounced onto the track ready to confront his enemy, but the train didn't flinch. So Tigger did what any cat worth his salt would do. He leapt straight up in the air, landed on the engine and rode it halfway around the track until he derailed it.

I thought he'd give up the chase after that, but he just couldn't leave it alone. A couple of days later, he attacked the train in the middle of the night and somehow turned it on.

All I know was that I was dead asleep when the whistle blew. I bolted out of bed in sheer panic. When I stumbled into the living room, I found the train on its side, wheels spinning and Tigger glaring at it from across the room.

That's when I yanked out the batteries and declared the Great Train War of 1996 officially over. If only all conflicts were so easy to resolve.

You might not have a mortal enemy this Christmas, but you might have someone who gets on your nerves. They know how to push your buttons and get under your skin. With so many family and friends around for the holidays it's easy to drive each other nuts.

Or perhaps you do have an enemy. Maybe someone who's hurt you or someone you've hurt. You might have a history with this person going back for years. It could be your ex or your boss or your neighbor. Doesn't really matter.

Like Tigger with the train, you just can't seem to let it go. You keep rehashing the past, reliving the pain and keeping olds wounds fresh. Not exactly a recipe for happy holidays, is it?

If only there were a way to take out the batteries and put an end to the whole thing. The Bible says there is. It's called forgiveness, and it's the first and best gift of Christmas. Jesus came to give it to you so you could pass it on to others.

Forgiveness drains our grudges of power, takes the steam out of our anger and even soothes the irritation of common annoyances. Most importantly it sets us free.

So what are you waiting for you? Whatever hurts you're holding onto, whether they're big or small, just let them go. Yank out the batteries and walk away. It will be the best gift you can give yourself this Christmas.

*Journal Prompts
for a Silent Night*

Have you asked God for His gift of forgiveness? If so, how did it feel to release that burden to Him?

Have you ever been forgiven by another person? How did it change the relationship when they let you off the hook?

Read Matthew 18:21-33. Is there anyone you're struggling to forgive? Who can help you pray through this process so you can finally be free?

God, thank you for forgiving me. Please help me to forgive others in the same way. I surrender my hurts, grudges and bitterness to you today.

Amen

16

THE NUTCRACKER TREE

You have turned my mourning into joyful dancing.

– PSALM 30:11 (NLT)

Every Christmas my daughters' ballet class performs the *Nut-cracker* just for parents. It's all impromptu. The teacher hands out parts on the spot and leads the kids through the story as they go.

When my youngest was five, she got stuck playing the Christmas tree. That meant she had to stand still while everyone else danced around her and decorated her with tinsel. Not exactly what she'd had in mind.

The year she turned six would different, she thought. This year was going to be her big break. She might get to play Clara or the Arabian Princess or even the Sugar Plum Fairy. She was dying to find out who she would be.

Unfortunately, she got the tree again.

Face tilted down, lip jutting out, she looked miserable. She didn't want to hold still. She didn't want to watch everyone else have fun. She wanted to dance.

Maybe that's you this Christmas. You ever feel like you've been stuck with a part you didn't want to play? Divorcee? Cancer patient? Grieving widow? Or maybe something else. Maybe you're caring for an aging parent or dealing with a rebellious child. Unemployed or on the edge of bankruptcy.

You didn't ask to play this part, but here you are, nonetheless, watching and waiting while everyone else gets to dance. Maybe next year will be different, you think. Maybe you'll finally get your big break. But you've thought that before, and nothing's changed.

It's tempting to blame God. After all, isn't He the one handing out the parts? Why do you keep getting stuck with the tree?

The truth is, however, that none of these crummy parts were in God's original dance. God hates death and sickness and heartbreak. There were no widows or orphans in His script, no one out of work, out of luck or out of options. But all of that changed in Eden.

When Adam and Eve turned their backs on God, they wrote new parts for us all, parts that involve tragedy, loneliness and struggle.

In Bethlehem, however, Jesus came to set it right. He entered the dance Himself and volunteered for the role that no one else could play. He took the part with the tree.

By His death, Jesus wrote a new ending to the story. He freed us to dance once again, not because our lives are trouble-free, but because we never dance alone.

God is with us. His power is available to us here and now. That means, despite what our circumstances tell us, we are never stuck. We are children of hope, free to dance with our Father who loves us.

Have you ever been stuck with a part in life you didn't want to play? What was it?

How did you feel about God in that season? Was it tough trust Him in the midst of hardship?

Read 2 Corinthians 4:16-18. What does this have to say about the difficult circumstances in our lives?

God, thanks for walking with me through the hardest seasons of life. Please help me to find joy and content-ment where I am today and trust you for my future.

Amen

17

THIS LITTLE LIGHT OF MINE

"In the same way, let your good deeds shine out for all to see,
so that everyone will praise your heavenly Father."

– MATTHEW 5:16 (NLT)

To be fair, we didn't set out to almost blow up a trailer court. It just kind of happened that way.

It was supposed to be a real Norman Rockwell kind of day. We'd gathered at church with several other couples to bake cookies for shut-ins and other folks who needed some Christmas cheer.

The baking part went great. We fired up the oven and turned the church kitchen into Santa's workshop, an operation that would have put the Keebler elves to shame. With flour and frosting flying we cranked out enough cookies to feed a third world country.

The place smelled like heaven.

It took the better part of the day, and by the time we'd finished, we had dozens of boxes packed with holiday goodies.

But the best was yet to come.

We weren't just going to drop the cookies and run. Oh no. We were going to treat our friends to a medley of good, old-fashioned

Christmas carols . . . by candlelight.

C'mon, caroling by candlelight? Unless your name happens to be Bing Crosby, you just can't get more festive than that.

To pull off this production, we had to work together like a well-oiled machine. Park the cars. Grab the cookies. Bust out the sheet music. Light the candles. Ring the doorbell. And let the magic begin!

At the first couple of houses everything went great. People were delighted and touched by the gesture. It was everything we were hoping for and more.

But then we arrived at the trailer court. That's where Charlie and Bertha lived.

Charlie was our church custodian, a sweet, older gentleman who took care of his ailing wife, Bertha. Bertha had a number of health problems that had kept her out of church for awhile, and we couldn't wait to let her know how much we loved her.

So, under the cover of darkness, we crept up to their mobile home, fired up our candles, and launched into our opening number.

Charlie answered the door and helped Bertha join us on her walker, her oxygen tank coming along for the ride. I can still remember the way their eyes misted up as we sang songs about the newborn King.

Charlie and Bertha were beautiful. Decades of faithful marriage. A lifetime of following Jesus. Hope overflowing even in the face of failing health. We all felt the power of that moment and realized they were blessing us way more than we could have blessed them. I wouldn't trade the memory of them standing in that doorway for anything.

But when I noticed the sign by the door, I knew it was time to wrap things up. By the soft glow of my candle, I read the words, "Danger! Oxygen in use. No smoking or open flame."

Hmm, I thought. I have an open flame. My wife has an open flame. All ten of us have open flames. And Bertha has enough oxygen to blow the whole trailer park to the North Pole and back.

Sorry folks, no time for an encore. It was time to douse those candles and call it a night.

Sometimes, in our clumsy efforts to share God's love with others, we all make mistakes. We say the wrong thing. We do the wrong thing. We make fools of ourselves and end up in all kinds of awkward situations.

And yes, from time-to-time, we may even almost blow up a trailer court or two.

But just because we don't love others perfectly, doesn't mean we shouldn't make the effort. You don't have to be an expert to show someone they matter to God. You just have to be available.

So this Christmas take a risk. Reach out to the lonely, the forgotten and those who just need a friend. Just make sure you follow state fire codes. And, you might want to leave the candles at home.

Have you ever tried to help someone but it didn't quite go according to plan?

Read 2 Corinthians 3:1-6. What does Paul say is the source of our competence?

Who needs you to take a risk and share God's love with them today?

God, thank you for the opportunity to love others. Help me to reach out to those who need to see you today and trust the results to you.

Amen

18

DREAMING OF A
WHITE ELEPHANT CHRISTMAS

Are you tired? Worn out? Burned out on religion?
Come to me. Get away with me and you'll recover your life . . .
Keep company with me and you'll learn to live freely and lightly.

– MATTHEW 11:28, 30 (MSG)

Have you ever been to a white elephant gift exchange? That's where you wrap up the worst item in your house in the hopes of unloading it on some poor sucker at Christmas. It's a prime opportunity to regift the most atrocious presents from Christmas past.

Got an Abraham Lincoln Chia Pet? A sweater with dogs playing poker? The Best of Liberace on 8-track? These are solid candidates for a white elephant party.

The worst white elephant gift I ever received was a plant stand shaped like a monkey. Not a cute, cartoonish monkey, but a strangely lifelike capuchin. It was the creepiest thing I've ever seen.

Still, I kept it in my office for years in the hopes that eventually I would get to pawn it off on someone else. Sure enough, I ended up at a white elephant party five years later, and the freaky, little monkey found itself a new home.

I like this white elephant tradition because it reminds me that

Christmas is about unloading burdens. It's about exchanging the things we were never meant to carry for gifts we could never earn.

Are you burdened by busyness this Christmas? God invites you to exchange it for rest. Weighed down by bitterness? Trade it in for forgiveness. Broken relationships? Swap them out for acceptance and love.

Yes, Jesus is in the white elephant business, taking the ugly pieces of our lives, the things we're desperate to be rid of and giving us a life of freedom in return. Not because He has to. But because He wants to. Because He loves us.

The prophet Isaiah described Jesus like this, "He was despised and rejected, a man of sorrows, acquainted with deepest grief . . . Yet it was our weakness he carried. It was our sorrows that weighed him down" (Isaiah 53:3-4 NLT).

It's not exactly the stuff of Christmas cards, yet deeply comforting just the same. Sure a baby in a manger is heart-warming, but a man of sorrows who carries our hurts? That's the gift we need.

Whatever burden you might be carrying this holiday season, it's time to give it away.

Journal Prompts
for a Silent Night

Have you ever been to a white elephant party? What did you give away and what did you receive?

What burdens are you carrying this Christmas? What's weighing down your heart?

Read Galatians 6:2. Is there anyone else you know who is carrying a heavy burden right now? How can you walk with them and help lighten their load?

God, please help me to release my burdens to you. Take my sin, my pain and my worries and replace them with freedom, healing and peace. I release it all to you now.

Amen

19

PINING AWAY

I am the true vine, and my Father is the gardener. He cuts
off every branch in me that bears no fruit, while every branch
that does bear fruit he prunes so that it will be even more fruitful.

– JOHN 15:1-2 (NIV)

The first time I took my daughter to a Christmas tree farm, she fell in love with the saplings. They were roped off to keep kids like mine from trampling them, but they were just too cute to resist.

"I want that one, Daddy!"

"We can't buy those," I said.

"Why not?"

"They're not for sale."

"Why not?"

"They've just been planted, " I said. "They need more time to grow."

This wasn't the answer she wanted to hear. She was ready to take her tiny tree home that day and cover it with bulbs and lights. Forget about the towering spruces or fragrant pines. The adorable little Charlie Brown tree had stolen her heart.

But even if I could have bought her that tree, you and I both know what would have happened. One ornament would have taken it to the ground. It just couldn't handle the weight.

No matter what I said, though, my daughter remained unconvinced. In her mind, the slender branches were more than ready. I know how she feels. Sometimes I see my life the same way my daughter saw those trees. I think I'm ready for things that God knows I'm clearly not mature enough to handle. I've always been this way, eager to jump into new adventures when I just needed to focus on the present moment and my own growth.

Can you relate? Have you ever wanted a promotion or a new job but kept getting overlooked? Are you ready to settle down and get married, but the right person just hasn't come along? Or maybe there's something else you're longing for in life and you wonder, "How long am I going to have to wait?"

The waiting is never easy. Just ask those Christmas trees. Think of the seasons of drought, the bitter winters and strong winds, the years of pruning and shaping, all that silent growing until some day they're strong enough to bear the light of Christmas.

Jesus called Himself the True Vine, the source of all spiritual nourishment and life. He compared His Father to a gardener who cuts away the dead branches of our lives and prunes the fruitful ones so that they will be even more fruitful in the end. But this pruning and waiting is painful business. True growth always is.

A mature Christmas tree is a beautiful thing, but they take years to grow. Same goes for a mature person. In the waiting seasons we grow stronger, more prepared for the challenges of life and ready to carry the light of Christ into the darkest places of the world.

Have you ever thought you were ready for something you later realized you weren't mature enough to handle yet?

What would have happened if God would have let you have it before you were ready?

Read John 15:1-8. How is God helping you grow right now? Is there anything He wants to prune back so you can be even more fruitful in the future?

God, thank you that my waiting is never wasted
with you. Thank you that you grow me during
these times to prepare me for my future. Help me
to be patient with the process and trust in you.

Amen

20

PLAYING SANTA

Let us not become weary in doing good, for at the proper time
we will reap a harvest if we do not give up.

– GALATIANS 6:9 (NIV)

Have you ever had someone throw cold water on your Christmas? Despite your best efforts to make the season merry and bright, sometimes you get nothing but a lump of coal in return.

I know how you feel. The year I dressed up as Santa, someone stole my pants. Bob Cratchett had his Scrooge. Cindy Lou Who had the Grinch. And I had the smart alec pants thief of 2010.

It all started when my boss asked me to play Santa at our staff Christmas party. In all due modesty, I rocked that Santa suit. Once you put on the costume, your jolly factor goes through the roof. I ho-ho-hoed with gusto, shook my belly like a bowl full of jelly and spread more Christmas cheer than Nat King Cole and Andy Williams rolled into one. I even had my own elves.

After opening with a rousing rendition of *Santa Claus Is Coming to Town*, the elves and I followed up with some witty, yuletide banter and brought down the house by distributing gifts. Yes, it was pure

Christmas magic, until I went to change back into my street clothes. That's when I discovered I'd been robbed.

Some comedian thought it would be funny to hide my jeans. This meant I had to stay in costume for the whole party and wait until the place cleared out to find my stolen pants. By that point it was just me, a few busboys and the poor lady who had to return the Santa suit to the costume shop.

I know what you're thinking. Why do bad things happen to good Santas? I guess that's just the way the Christmas cookie crumbles. No matter how hard we may try to make Christmas special for those around us, we can't control how they will respond. Our thoughtful gifts may go unappreciated. Our family gatherings may be nothing but drama. We may go out of our way to help someone and find ourselves misunderstood, rejected or wondering why we even went to the trouble.

But don't lose heart. That's how Christmas giving has gone down since Bethlehem. When Jesus arrived in the manger, only a handful of people received Him as a gift from God. Most ignored Him. Crazy king Herod even tried to kill Him. "He came into the very world he created, but the world didn't recognize him. He came to his own people, and even they rejected him" (John 1:10-11 NLT).

Yet, Jesus continued to love people, give generously and sacrifice Himself for others no matter how people responded to Him. This Christmas how could we do any less?

We can't control how people react to us. We can only control ourselves. We can choose to be gracious or we can let the immaturity of others shape us into cynics. As for me, I say we continue to play Santa despite the Scrooges, Grinches and pants thieves who may try to steal our Christmas joy.

Journal Prompts
for a Silent Night

Have you ever performed an act of kindness only to be met with rejection? How did you respond?

Who are the people who are the most challenging for you to love right now? Are you ever tempted to give up trying?

When have you been difficult to love? Who are the people who never gave up on you during that season?

God, you know what it's like to be rejected, but that never stopped you from loving people. Help me to keep serving others no matter how they react.

Amen

21

THE GIVER OF ALL GOOD THINGS

*Every good and perfect gift is from above,
coming down from the Father of the heavenly lights,
who does not change like shifting shadows.*

— JAMES 1:17 (NIV)

When my cousin Ted was a kid, he asked for an Atari 2600 for Christmas, but his dad wrapped up a box of bricks instead. Sometimes dads think they're funny when they're not. You see, the Atari wasn't just a big deal that Christmas. It was THE big deal.

Launched at the height of the arcade craze of the 70's, the Atari 2600 was the first major home video game system, and we all wanted one. We had no Wii, Xbox or Play Station so the Christmas hopes and dreams of millions of kids were pinned on the 2600. For the first time in history you could have an arcade in your living room just like that kid on Silver Spoons.

Ted was convinced he was getting an Atari. The box looked like an Atari. It felt like an Atari, but when he tore into it on Christmas morning, he discovered the devastating truth—nothing but bricks and newspaper. No console. No joysticks. No game cartridges. No dream come true.

Thankfully, the Atari was in the other room, and Ted's dad was just messing with him. Like I said, sometimes dads think they're funny. After Ted started to cry, they brought out the real present, played a game of Combat and all was forgiven.

Of course there had to be an Atari in this story, right? It's one thing to tease a kid, but what kind of a dad would actually give his child bricks when he asked for a video game?

Jesus once asked a similar question to describe what His Father is like. He said, "You parents—if your children ask for a loaf of bread, do you give them a stone instead? Or if they ask for a fish, do you give them a snake? Of course not! So if you sinful people know how to give good gifts to your children, how much more will your heavenly Father give good gifts to those who ask him" (Matthew 7:9-11 NLT).

Think about that. Most of us who are parents try to do right by our kids. We love them, provide for them and enjoy surprising them with gifts whenever possible. Generosity is the natural posture of a parent's heart toward their child—even for imperfect parents like us.

Now consider God, the perfect Father. Not an ounce of selfishness in His being. Imagine how much He must long to provide for His children. Imagine how He must love to give good gifts to His kids if only we would take the time to ask.

That doesn't mean God is our genie in heaven, but it does mean He is for us, and we can trust Him with our wants and needs. It means that He wants us to express our desires to Him and then have faith that He will work things out for our ultimate good.

Of course, our ultimate good is to become like Jesus. Our ultimate good involves the transformation of our character and heart. Sometimes that road is painful, but it doesn't mean God is sticking us with a box of bricks. It just means He has something better waiting for us in the next room.

Even in the midst of hardship, God is our Dad in heaven, and He is the giver of all good things.

Have you ever been disappointed with God? Did it cause you to doubt His character?

Read Romans 8:28. How can God use even the hard times in our lives for our good?

What are the some of God's good gifts you're thankful for today? Make a list and tell Him how grateful you are.

God, you are a good Dad. Thank you for your generosity in my life. Please help me to trust in your character as I lay my wants and needs before you today.

Amen

22

RECEIVING CHRISTMAS

Yet to all who did receive him, to those who believed in his name,
he gave the right to become children of God.

– JOHN 1:12 (NIV)

During the holiday season, someone is sure to remind you that it's more blessed to give than receive. To be totally honest, though, sometimes it's actually easier too. Have you ever received a gift so awful you didn't know how to react?

My friend Laura insists on knowing what presents she's receiving before she opens them. It's not because she's greedy. She just wants to be polite. She has a terrible poker face. The only way she can adequately prepare herself is by finding out what she's getting in advance.

If you're like Laura, you might find it challenging when you open a present that's not quite right for you. But other times it's just as difficult to open an amazing gift, a gift so thoughtful that you just can't find the words to express your gratitude. How do you react to a gift like that?

The struggle to receive gifts well is nothing new. Just look at the nativity story. When God announced the gift of His Son, Mary was greatly troubled. Joseph was ready to call off the wedding. The people of Jerusalem were freaking out, and Herod brought in the hit squad.

Two thousand years ago, God gave mankind the greatest gift of all time, and no one knew what to do with Him. Sometimes we still don't. The cynical dismiss Him as a fraud. The political use Him to gain power. The busy blow Him off in the hurry of holiday preparations.

But others—the humble, the broken and the desperate—they know how to receive with empty hands, open hearts and overwhelming gratitude that defines the rest of their lives.

John 1:12 says, "Yet to all who did receive him, to those who believed in his name, he gave the right to become children of God" (NIV).

Jesus isn't just the reason for the season. He's the proof that God is crazy about you. He's the proof that the One who sees you at your worst still believes in the potential of your best. Fresh starts and clean slates are the order of the day in heaven, where God generously bestows gifts of forgiveness and endless life.

Sure it's more blessed to give than receive, but we have to receive first before we have anything of real worth to give. If you want to give your loved ones the best Christmas ever, start by receiving the best gift ever—the unconditional, unbelievable, yet undeniable love of God freely available in Jesus.

Journal Prompts
for a Silent Night

Do you find it easier to gift gifts or receive them? Why?

What's the most memorable gift you've ever given?
What's the most memorable gift you've ever received?

Have you received the gift of a relationship with Jesus in your life? If not, what's holding you back? If so, have you made space to receive His love in a fresh way today?

God, thank you for the gift of your Son.
Help me to receive Him into my life today with empty
hands, an open heart and overwhelming gratitude.

Amen

23

CHRISTMAS INSIDE THE BOX

*This will be a sign to you: You will find a baby
wrapped in cloths and lying in a manger.*

– LUKE 2:12 (NIV)

Every Christmas I obsess over boxes. It's because I'm a last minute shopper. By the time I get around to wrapping presents, my wife has already used every gift box in our house, which means I have to get creative. I'm not above using cereal boxes, tissue boxes and everything short of the cat's litter box to get my presents wrapped. If I'm pressed for time, however, nothing is off limits.

That means if you get a present from me it might not come in the original package. So don't get too excited about that box of Lucky Charms because there might be something entirely different inside. Boxes are tricky like that. The simplest packages may contain the most extraordinary gifts.

In Christian circles people say you can't put God in a box. By that they mean you can't limit God. Sometimes He does things you would never expect Him to do, love people you'd never expect Him to love, forgive people you'd never expect Him to forgive, that sort of thing.

They also mean He's not a Baptist God, a Methodist God, a Catholic God, a Republican God or a Democrat God. He's just God, and He was God long before we were around to label Him.

In that respect, yes, it's true. You can't put God in a box, but on Christmas, God did it to Himself. He put Himself in a box called a manger. We cannot limit God, but in Bethlehem God limited Himself—all the fullness of Deity crammed into infant flesh.

Boxes are helpful things. You can get your arms around them. You can carry them with You. You can even give them away. That's the beauty of Jesus. He is God wrapped up in a way that we can see Him, hear Him, touch Him and even give Him away to others.

Cosmic, almighty God? It's tough to get my head around that, but Jesus, walking around loving people? That, I can see. That, with His power, I can even begin to do.

This God in a box, who we call Jesus, is a gift we can unwrap each day as we spend time with Him and come to know Him better. So go ahead, open the box and prepare to be delighted. He is all you could want and more.

Journal Prompts
for a Silent Night

Have you ever seen someone try to place limits on what they think God would or wouldn't do or the kind of people He would or wouldn't love? Have you tried to put God in a box yourself?

Why do you think God limited Himself by becoming a human? What can you discover about God by looking at the life of Jesus?

What can you do this week to unwrap the gift of Jesus and get to know Him better this Christmas season?

God, thank you for putting yourself in that manger so many years ago. Thank you for taking on flesh so I can see you and know you and make you known.

Amen

24

GINGERBREAD SWEATSHOP

He will wipe every tear from their eyes,
and there will be no more death or sorrow or crying or pain.
All these things are gone forever.

– REVELATION 21:4 (NLT)

Making a gingerbread house is fun. Making eighteen gingerbread houses is insane. Yet, that's what I found myself doing to prepare for my daughter's eighth birthday party just a few weeks before Christmas.

Since her birthday is right in the middle of the holiday season, my wife decided to throw her a snow-themed party with all kinds of wintery activities for her guests. Best of all, each girl would get to decorate her very own gingerbread house.

Of course, the girls wouldn't actually have time to construct the houses themselves, just decorate them. That meant someone would need to assemble all of the gingerbread houses in advance. That someone, my wife informed me, would be me.

No problem, I thought. Slap together a few houses and I'd be done. That shouldn't take long. Turns out it was more than a few. Every girl my daughter invited to her party decided to come. The next thing I knew we'd converted our kitchen into a gingerbread sweatshop, and I would not be allowed to leave until the job was done.

With Christmas music blasting, I mixed up bowl after bowl of frosting, cut out walls with a serrated knife and assembled 108 pieces into 18 houses. I even decorated an extra house as an example to give the kids some ideas of what they might do.

By the end I was crummy, sticky, exhausted mess. Our kitchen looked like Willie Wonka's chocolate factory had just exploded, spewing candy and frosting everywhere.

However, when the kids arrived for the party the next day, none of that mattered. Their faces lit up like Christmas trees when they saw the gingerbread city that covered our dining room table. But what truly made it special was that in the midst of that sugary wonderland, nestled between the bowls of M&Ms, gumdrops and marshmallows, each girl found a tiny house that had been prepared just for her.

This Christmas Jesus wants you to know that you're invited to a party too. It is a sweet celebration where God and His people will be together at last, and at that party, you will find a home prepared just for you.

Jesus once told His friends, "There is more than enough room in my Father's home. If this were not so, would I have told you that I am going to prepare a place for you? When everything is ready, I will come and get you, so that you will always be with me where I am" (John 14:2-3 NLT).

Each Christmas we have the opportunity to celebrate not only the Savior who came long ago, but the Savior who will one day come again. When He does, He will kick off a party that will never end. I don't know about you, but I can't wait to see what He has planned.

I doubt there will be a gingerbread city, but there will be the city of God, where we will once again experience the wide-eyed wonder of children who have stepped in a world of joy.

Journal Prompts
for a Silent Night

How would you describe the perfect home?

What do you think heaven's going to be like?

Read Revelation 21:1-5. What are you looking forward to the most about the day Jesus returns?

God, thank you for preparing a home for me in heaven. I cannot wait to see what you have planned. As I celebrate Bethlehem, help me to eagerly look forward to the day you come again.

Amen

25

LOST AND FOUND

When they saw the star, they were overjoyed. On coming
to the house, they saw the child with his mother Mary,
and they bowed down and worshiped him.

– MATTHEW 2:10-11 (NIV)

When it comes to holiday road trips, there's a lot that can go wrong. Just ask Stuart Fish's family. According to an article in *USA Today*, the Fish family drove over 1,000 miles to spend Christmas with family in Utah, but on their journey, something terrible happened.

They lost a gift. Not just any gift, mind you, but the big gift on Stuart's wish list, a LEGO MINDSTORMS robot. They weren't sure how it happened, but somewhere along the road, it fell out of their truck, apparently never to be seen again.

But Christmas is a season of miracles, and a few weeks after the Fish family returned home to Minnesota, they received the surprise of their lives. It turned out that a Highway Patrol Trooper, named Jared Clanton, had spotted their package beside the road and had been using his best detective skills to track them down.

He didn't have much to go on, except for the name of the toy store on the box, but when Stuart's mom went to buy a new robot for Stuart's birthday, the store owner made the connection.

When Officer Clanton got the call, he shipped the present to Stuart at his own expense, along with ten dollars and a note that said, "Stuart, buddy, I heard you lost something but you didn't know what it was. I also heard it's your birthday as well, so Happy Birthday."[9]

It's easy to lose a gift on the road to Christmas. Perhaps you've lost something too. It's a long journey through the month of December, and in the busyness of the season much may be misplaced. Perhaps you've lost the gift of peace or joy or wonder or hope. Or like Stuart, maybe you don't even know what you've lost along the way. Yet, you feel like something is missing.

Thankfully, there is a God who is already on the case, a God who will meet you on the holiday road and help you to find the gifts that He made for you to enjoy. Over the pages of this book I hope I've pointed you back to Him and that you are well on your way to rediscovering the lost joys of the Christmas season.

Like the wise men who sought Jesus on that first holiday road trip long ago, you are sure to find Him if you don't give up. As the prophet Jeremiah reminds us, "You will seek me and find me when you seek me with all your heart" (Jeremiah 29:13 NIV).

May your journey be sweet and your soul be blessed as you keep on traveling the holiday road.

Journal Prompts for a Silent Night

What gift is God helping you rediscover this Christmas? Peace? Wonder? Joy? Hope?

What does it look like for you to seek Jesus with all of your heart?

Which Bible verse in this devotional has been most meaningful to you along the holiday road? Write it down somewhere you'll see it regularly to keep it fresh in your mind.

God, thank you for Jesus. Help me to seek Him above all else today and show me how to reclaim the good gifts of Christmas I may have lost along the way.

Amen

BONUS SECTION

Holiday Devotions throughout the Year

26

New Year's Day

NEW YEAR'S OPPOLUTIONS

My grace is sufficient for you,
for my power is made perfect in weakness.

– 2 CORINTHIANS 12:9 (NIV)

Are you tired of starting off January with good intentions that never become reality? Are you sick of feeling like a failure just because you lack discipline and willpower? Do you want to make resolutions for the new year that actually work? Then I have a strategy that's just for you. I call them New Year's oppolutions.

What are New Year's oppolutions? I'm glad you asked. New Year's oppolutions are based on the fact that next to no one actually follows through on their New Year's resolutions. In fact we often end up doing the exact opposite of the good we intend to do. So instead of wallowing in that failure, I say let's put that principle to work on our behalf.

Whatever goal you'd like to accomplish in the new year, simply resolve to do the opposite. For example, do you want to start eating healthier? Then set a goal of eating a dozen Krispy Kreme doughnuts a day. C'mon, we all know you can't actually stick to a New Year's resolution. You'll be chowing down on nothing but broccoli and carrots by Valentine's Day.

Want to get control of your finances? Make a resolution to apply for a new credit card each week and max it out. Before you know it, not only will you be debt-free but you'll be saving up a sizable nest egg for retirement.

How about kicking the nicotine habit? No problem. Resolve to smoke three times as much as last year, maybe even multiple cigarettes at once. Try to see how many fists full of cigarettes you can actually fit in your mouth at the same time. With that kind of goal, you'll say so long to smoking in no time flat.

Okay, so maybe that's a bad idea. Maybe using reverse psychology on ourselves wouldn't be all that effective. Why? Because none of us ever struggled to carry through on bad choices. We could keep unhealthy resolutions all day long. It's only when we vow to do good that our willpower tends to diminish. The apostle Paul put it like this, "I don't really understand myself, for I want to do what is right, but I don't do it. Instead, I do what I hate" (Romans 7:15 NLT).

I've lived that Bible verse more times than I care to admit. I've resolved to make changes in my life and failed over and over again. I know exactly what Paul means when he throws his hands up in exasperation and declares, "Oh, what a miserable person I am" (Romans 7:24 NLT).

Fortunately for us, the story doesn't end there. The good news is that there is a God who can free us from a life of frustration and failure. In fact, people who are frustrated and failing are God's specialty.

It's in our failure that we give up control, get out of the way and finally give God room to work. That's why the only New Year's resolution worth making is to stop trying and to start trusting. The sooner we stop trying to overcome our bad habits, selfishness and unhealthy tendencies on our own, the sooner we can start trusting God to do the heavy lifting that we never could.

In our hopelessness we discover hope. In our weakness we discover God's strength. In our failure we find victory. The kingdom of God is full of wonderful paradoxes like these that open the door to freedom and growth. Instead of New Year's oppolutions, God offers New Year's opportunities to experience the full life He made us to enjoy.

27

Snow Day

UNEXPECTED HOLIDAY

Purify me from my sins, and I will be clean;
wash me, and I will be whiter than snow.

– PSALM 51:7 (NLT)

When you're a kid, nothing beats the magic of a snow day, especially one you don't expect. The best ones are a total surprise. I can remember going to sleep in elementary school with no hope of snow but waking up to a world buried under a blanket of white.

Snow days got me out of tests I was dreading and saved me from having to face the music for unfinished homework. It was like a reprieve from the executioner, a get-out-of-jail-free card delivered by Jack Frost.

On snow days the world was new, transformed from a place of everyday routine to a glistening wonderland of adventure. Sledding, snowmen, snow forts, snow ice cream and snowball fights of epic proportion were the order of the day.

Snow days were nothing but grace. The natural order of things had been turned upside-down. What should have happened didn't happen. And what happened instead was awesome!

I think about days like this when I read the promise God offers me each morning that He will take the stains of my selfishness and my sin and make them, "as white as snow" (Isaiah 1:18 NLT).

I don't know about you but left to my own I tend to make a mess of things. I've fumbled relationships, made stupid choices and put myself first more times than I care to remember.

But then one day I woke up to an unbelievable surprise. Not only was there a God who loved me but who loved me enough to take my heart and wipe it clean. Instead of being rejected by God I was accepted and drawn near.

I was given a snow day, where all my mistakes were covered in a fresh blanket of forgiveness.

What should have happened didn't happen. And what happened instead was awesome.

I don't know what you're dreading today or regretting from the past, but I do know that God offers snow days each and every day, an opportunity for a clean slate and a new start. Does that surprise you? The best snow days usually do.

So what are you waiting for? Put on some mittens, grab your sled and head out into the wonderland of God's amazing grace.

28

Groundhog Day

STUCK IN YOUR OWN GROUNDHOG DAY

So if the Son sets you free, you will be free indeed.

– JOHN 8:36 (NIV)

You ever feel like you're living in the movie *Groundhog Day?* That's the one where Bill Murray plays arrogant weatherman Phil Conner, who gets stuck in time in Punxsutawney, Pennsylvania, where every day is Groundhog Day. Over the course of the film, Conner is forced to relive the same day over and over and over again.

In the real world, we're probably not going to find ourselves trapped in a magical time loop like Conner, but we may feel just as stuck.

For you that might mean reliving the same day over and over in your mind. It could be a day of trauma or regret. It may be a day tainted by words you can't take back, mistakes you can't undo, or pain inflicted on you by someone else. No matter how hard you try, you just can't seem to get past that day.

Or maybe the day you're reliving is a happy day. Treasuring the positive experiences of life can lead to thankfulness and joy. However, nostalgia can also be a subtle trap that makes us bitter. We may find ourselves pining for the "good old days" instead of living the life God has given us here and now.

Some of us, though, aren't stuck in the past. We're stuck in the present. We keep making the same mistakes, chasing the same addictions or falling into the same kinds of unhealthy relationships that have plagued us for years. The names and faces might change, but we're living out the same old situations time and time again.

But maybe that's not you. You're not stuck in the past or the present. You're stuck in the future. You're trapped in a day that hasn't even happened yet, a day that may never happen. Do you worry about your kids' future? Are you scared about growing older? Are you dreading what's coming down the road? If so, you may be as stuck as Phil Conner, consumed by worries and what-ifs, trapped by the power of your own anxiety.

The great news, though, is that we don't have to be stuck. Not in the past. Not in the future. Not in the present. We can be free of regret, free of anxiety, and free to choose our destiny each and every moment. How? Well, not like they do it in the movies.

In *Groundhog Day*, Phil Conner grew to be a better person, and it was this change that finally set him free. Eventually, Conner learned to be kind and selfless, and, as a result, worthy of love.

But real life doesn't work like that. It's better. In real life, we are not set free because we become the best version of ourselves. We are set free so we can become the best version of ourselves.

God doesn't love us when we finally get it right. He loves us when we can't get it right. He loves us even when we're at our worst. That's called grace, and grace always leads to freedom.

When we invite God into our lives, freedom is sure to follow. 2 Corinthians 3:17 says it like this, "where the Spirit of the Lord is, there is freedom" (NIV).

How does God set us free? He forgives our past and empowers us to forgive others. He secures our future, liberating us from worry and dread. He even breaks the chains of the present that keep us repeating the same old mistakes.

So if you find yourself stuck today, don't settle for a world where it's always Groundhog Day. Ask God to help you make a change. Ask him for wise friends to give you good counsel. Ask him for the power and courage to finally move on, and step into a bright new day.

29

Valentine's Day

THE BIGGEST VALENTINE

We love because he first loved us.

– 1 JOHN 4:19 (NIV)

When my daughter had her first Valentine's Day party at school, they had a rule that said you had to bring cards for every kid in the class. It ensured that no one went home empty handed or felt left out.

I don't remember such a rule when I was a kid. During my childhood, Valentine's Day was a social report card that showed you how many people actually liked you. Even if you did give valentines to the entire class, there were subtle tricks you could pull to communicate more value to your closest friends.

The first thing you could do was reserve the primo valentines in the pack for your best pals or potential sweethearts. For example, if I gave out Star Wars valentines that year, and you got a Luke or Vader, you were in my inner circle. However, if I gave you a random creature from the Mos Eisley cantina, that was just a courtesy card. And Princess Leia? Well, that meant you were one lucky girl.

The other thing you could do to upgrade your valentines was

to tape a sucker to the card or give a bigger card to certain people. In some cultures, that's actually considered a proposal of marriage. But Valentine's Day wasn't just a day to give cards. It was also a day to receive. I remember our whole class working hard coloring hearts on brown, paper bags to serve as mailboxes. Once the mailboxes were done, we would leave them on our desk and mill about the room delivering our cards.

When I returned to my mailbox, it was time to face the truth. How did I do? How many valentines did I get, and how high on the social pecking order did they register? Did any of my special valentine friends reciprocate with awesome cards or did they leave me hanging with an awkward snub?

It's funny to remember how big of a deal this was as a kid, but for some of us, this quest for love never ends. Many of us, even as adults, waste too much time craving the affirmation of others. It's like we're still carrying around that brown, paper bag waiting for the people around us to fill it with words or gestures of love.

When someone's mad at you, it ruins your day. If you see your friends having fun on Facebook without you, you feel rejected. If you did something great for your spouse, but they failed to make a big deal out of it, you think they don't appreciate you.

But here's the secret about that brown, paper mailbox. It has a big, fat hole in the bottom. No matter how happy you make people, and no matter how much affirmation you receive in return, it will never, ever be enough. It never lasts.

Thankfully, there is a different kind of love, a sufficient, abundant overflowing love that speaks value into you that no one can take away. It is the love of God. And it says you are cherished. You are beloved. You are treasured.

Jesus' friend John wrote these words long ago, "See how very much our Father loves us, for he calls us his children, and that is what we are" (1 John 3:1 NLT).

So whether it's Valentine's Day or any other day, stop waiting on other people to fill you with self-worth. It's time to throw away that paper bag. There is a Valentine message that trumps all others, and it says unequivocally that you are already loved more than you can possibly imagine.

30

Easter

HUNTING EASTER

Jesus said to her, "I am the resurrection and the life.
Those who believe in me will have life even if they die.

– JOHN 11:25 (NCV)

When I was a kid, I had a bloodhound nose for hunting Easter Eggs. It's like I could smell the vinegar in the egg dye. I'd make my parents hide them for weeks leading up to Easter and as far beyond as I could milk it.

As an egg-hunting purist I insisted on using hard-boiled eggs I'd colored myself, though the plastic ones would do in a pinch. Weather never stopped me. Even on rainy, spring days, we'd hide eggs inside.

On one of those days, I got carried away and hid an egg a little too well. We found it sometime around the Fourth of July. At that point even an amateur could have sniffed it out. If I close my eyes, I think I can still smell it.

My wife's family didn't just hide her eggs. They hid her Easter basket too. I'd never heard of that one. She claims it was fun to look for it, but I suspect she'll end up in counseling. No one should hide chocolate. It's just wrong.

I guess Easter, though, has always been about hiding things.

After Jesus was dead and buried, his friends hid in a locked room, afraid the same thing would happen to them. The hope they'd once had lay hidden in a hillside tomb. And where was God when their dreams fell apart? He seemed to be hiding too.

God's good at that sometimes.

I spent one Easter several years ago waiting to see if I had a brain tumor. Something weird had come back on a routine test, and my doctor just wanted to make sure it was nothing. I asked him what he was looking for, and he said, "Oh you know, it could be a tumor."

Like Arnold Schwarzenegger in the film *Kindergarten Cop* I kept telling myself, "It's not a too-mah." Still, anxiety has a funny way of creeping in because we all know life comes with few guarantees. I had a two-year-old daughter at the time and a second one on the way.

I felt like Jesus' friends in the locked room. I was stuck. All I could do was wait.

God seemed to be doing His Easter egg bit. Hiding. Silent.

As I waited to hear from the doctor, I had to teach hundreds of families at a special Easter event at my church. I must have gone over the resurrection story dozens of times preparing to speak, and the more times I read it, the more a persistent thought began to stab at my fear.

I follow a guy who walked out of a tomb. Why am I worried?

That did it for me. I'd found my Easter egg. Empty graves trump test results every time. I knew in that moment that whatever the doctor told me would be okay.

A few weeks later I got good news from the doctor, and though I was thrilled, it paled in comparison with the good news God had already given me. Jesus is alive, and I'm alive with Him. Now and forever.

This Easter, I'm sure I'll hide my fair share of eggs. After all, my daughters have inherited my blood-hound nose. And every time we play this game of hide and seek, I'm going to remember the hidden God who loves to be found and the sheer joy of the hope of Easter.

31

Mother's Day

THE BEAR FACTS ABOUT MOMS

Can a mother forget her nursing child?
Can she feel no love for the child she has borne?
But even if that were possible, I would not forget you!

– ISAIAH 49:15 (NLT)

One year while driving through the mountains in Tennessee, I saw a bunch of cars pulled over on the side the road. Where were all the passengers? Standing around the base of a tree several hundred yards away. What was in the tree? A cute little bear cub nestled in a crook near the top. Where was I? Videoing the whole thing from the safety of my car.

I'm no park ranger, but I've watched enough Animal Planet to know that wherever you find a bear cub, Mama Bear can't be far behind. And believe me, you do not want to get caught between the two. Why? Because Mama Bear will tear you to shreds. That's just how Mama Bears roll. Nobody gets between them and their cubs.

I know how this works. I'm married.

After nine years of marriage, I thought I knew everything there was to know about my wife. Then we had our first baby, and I got to see Christy in a whole new light. I got to see her as a mom. This was a total game changer.

I've been amazed at both the depths of her tenderness towards our girls, and her Mama Bear fierceness when she senses a threat. When my daughters get sick, she turns into Florence Nightengale. When they're threatened, she turns into the Incredible Hulk. It's both heart-warming and frightening.

It's also a lot like God. We talk about God being a Father, which is how the Bible often describes Him, but there's also a Mama Bear side to God that I've been able to understand better by watching the moms in my life protect their kids.

The prophet Hosea once described God as a raging mother bear robbed of her cubs. His people had turned away from Him and were chasing things that would inevitably lead to their destruction.

So, how did God react? It was go time. The gloves were off. Nothing would stop Him from bringing His lost cubs back home, and Heaven help anyone or anything who tried to stand in the way.

There are times when I turn my back on God and try to do life on my own. Yes, God gently invites me to return to His loving arms. But sometimes He growls too. Sometimes He shreds my best laid plans and all the things I think will satisfy my heart without Him. Sometimes He thwarts me. Sometimes He stops me. Sometimes He makes life downright hard. Why? Because that's how Mama Bears roll.

Their fierce love will shred anything that stands between them and their cubs.

This Mother's Day I'm not just going to think about God's tender and nurturing side that is reflected in the gentleness of so many great moms in my life. I'm also going to think about the savage protectiveness of the Mama Bear God, and how thankful I am for His unstoppable love.

32

Father's Day

SUPER DAD

See how very much our Father loves us,
for he calls us his children, and that is what we are!

– 1 JOHN 3:1 (NLT)

A few weeks ago, I posted this question on Facebook, "What's the first word that comes to mind when you hear the word dad?" Some people responded with single word answers like unshakable, trustworthy, and love.

Still others had to elaborate even more, as if one word couldn't sum up their memories of their fathers. Here's what they said:

"Strength. He would protect his family no matter what. Nothing could stop him."

"Magical. He could fix anything and make the scary monsters in my room disappear."

"Dependable. Always there no matter what the reason is."

"Protector . . . especially if I had a scary dream."

"I don't have a word that comes to mind, but instead a picture of holding hands with my dad."

"I can picture him on our tractor mowing . . . cutting wood in the fall to heat our home through the winter."

"Soft shoe dancing wherever and whenever the music hits."

These memories that my friends shared reminded me of how many great dads there are out there. Sometimes that's easy to forget because fathers get so much bad press.

So many stories you hear about dads are negative, many justly so. You hear about dads ditching their families, abusing their kids or just being an all around jerk. I've watched grown men and women weep over the relationship they wish they'd had with their fathers but never could. It seems like no one has the capacity to mess up a person's life like a dad.

Yet, those Facebook comments also show me that few people have the capacity to bless a kid like their dad. For so many of us our dads were Superman. I know mine definitely was for me. Still is.

He was the strongest guy in the world. Even though I had a wild imagination and could picture a boogeyman around every corner, I always felt safe with my dad, and I always felt loved.

That's why it was so easy for me to follow God as an adult. My relationship with my dad on earth prepared me for my relationship with a Dad in heaven. Some people aren't so lucky. It's hard for some of you to think of God as a perfect Father because your dad was less than what you needed him to be.

I'm genuinely sorry for that. And God is too.

I think the reason people are so disappointed with absent or abusive fathers is that deep down we sense we were made for a relationship with a different kind of dad. When you don't get that as a kid, you feel ripped off. Maybe you even convince yourself you never needed a dad in the first place.

If that's the boat you're in, I understand. It makes total sense, but I'd also encourage you to not let a crummy dad on earth cheat you out of friendship with an incredible Dad in heaven.

Father's Day is the perfect time to celebrate the dads who got it right and to forgive the dads who didn't. But even better than that, it's the chance to embrace the one Dad who will never leave you, never hurt you and will always be the Father you need.

33

Fourth of July

THE PURSUIT OF HAPPINESS

Seek the Kingdom of God above all else, and live righteously,
and he will give you everything you need.

– MATTHEW 6:33 (NLT)

There are few things more American than a small town 4th of July parade. Cars decked out in crepe paper. Folks lining the streets waving flags. And candy. Buckets of candy.

Have you seen how people throw this stuff out? It's like chumming the water for sharks. Once the feeding frenzy begins, it doesn't take long to escalate into a all-out candy apocalypse.

A couple of years ago our family was hanging out with some friends watching one of these fiascos. My friend's preschool son, Riley, was having trouble getting candy. The big kids kept jumping out in front of him and picking the pavement clean before he even had a chance.

But then his dad noticed there were a few pieces in the road nearby. One float had already passed us, and there was a big gap in the parade so his dad told him, "Riley, go get it. Go get the candy."

Apparently, Riley didn't see the candy on the street. He took off at a full sprint chasing the last float down the road. I've never seen a kid run so fast. He wasn't just going to settle for one piece of the candy. He was going straight to the source.

He probably made it a good fifty feet before his dad bolted after him. This kid was not turning back. He was taking Thomas Jefferson's "pursuit of happiness" line from the Declaration of Independence seriously. Fists pumping, legs flying, Riley was pursuing the source of his happiness with all of his might.

I have a lot to learn from that.

Too many times I've settled for the candy in the street. The stray pieces. The leftovers. The little things I thought would make me happy, but soon left me hungry for more.

Achievements? Approval? Possessions? Not bad by themselves, but when I count on those to satisfy me, I'm disappointed every time. The flavor wears out faster than five cent gum, and I'm left looking for the next thing that can do the trick.

But if I take my cue from Riley and run straight to the source, that's a different story altogether. Jesus' brother James once wrote, "Whatever is good and perfect is a gift coming down to us from God" (James 1:17 NLT).

The God who invented chocolate and beaches and laughter is a God worth knowing. The pleasures He's created are simply a reflection of the character and nature of God Himself. And even if the circumstances of my life rob me of enjoying what God's created, they can never stop me from enjoying God.

The pursuit of happiness is great and all, but the pursuit of God leads to a deep and lasting joy.

34

Halloween

WHAT ARE YOU GOING TO BE?

> Don't copy the behavior and customs
> of this world, but let God transform you
> into a new person by changing the way you think.

– ROMANS 12:2 (NLT)

It was never about the candy. Never. Candy was just an excuse. It gave us a reason to trick-or-treat. Never once, though, did another kid ask me, "What kind of chocolate are you going to get this year?"

Instead, we asked the other question, the magic question. What are you going to be this year? Not, what are you going to wear? What are you going to be?

When we were kids, we didn't just put on costumes. We took on new identities. We transformed, and every October the possibilities were endless.

I became Batman, Superman, Zorro and Darth Vader among others. I didn't just walk from house to house. I flew. I galloped. I zoomed across town in the Batmobile. For a night, I wasn't just a chubby kid with homework and glasses. I was whatever I wanted to be. Heroic. Powerful. Awesome.

Afterwards, it didn't matter that I had to go back to being my

121

normal old self for the next eleven months. I had a bucket full of candy as a consolation prize, and Christmas was just around the corner. But more than that, I knew October would eventually come around again, and the stores would restock their shelves with those costume boxes, the ones with the plastic windows on the lids that served as gateways to another world.

Once more my friends and I would ask the question, "What are you going to be?"

At some point, though, I stopped believing in the magic of masks and vinyl suits. Unfortunately, I didn't just give up the childhood fantasy of Halloween, but also the underlying truth that made it so powerful.

I stopped believing in the miracle of transformation. I stopped believing I could become something other than what I am today.

How about you? Did you have big dreams as a kid, but now those dreams don't seem possible? Are there areas of your life you wish you could change, but don't believe you can?

I'll never lose this weight. I'll never get out of debt. I'll never have the courage to say no. I'll never start my own business. I'll never escape my past. I'll never kick this addiction. I'll never forgive him. I'll never make this marriage work. I'll never amount to anything. I'll never get my act together. I'll never be happy.

The word never is a padlock on our future. It says I am this and not that, and nothing will ever change it. But the good news is there is a God who holds the key to that lock. He is the God of possibilities who blows away our nevers like a house of cards.

Just ask David, a backwoods shepherd boy who God turned into a king. Or Zacchaeus, a crook who became the most generous man in town. Or Peter, a lying coward transformed into a hero of faith.

Paul, a guy who had his own life turned upside-down by God, explains it like this, "God can do anything, you know—far more than you could ever imagine or guess or request in your wildest dreams! He does it not by pushing us around but by working within us, his Spirit deeply and gently within us" (Ephesians 3:20 MSG).

When it comes to your future, God doesn't believe in nevers. He believes in you. He's still young enough and playful enough to believe in the miracle of transformation and that you can become anything He wants you to be.

So wherever you feel stuck, whatever seems impossible to change, turn it over to Him. He's waiting like a kid on Halloween to ask you that magic question. What are you going to be this year? What are you going to be?

35

Thanksgiving

THE BIRTHDAY THAT ATE THANKSGIVING

*Be thankful in all circumstances, for this is God's will
for you who belong to Christ Jesus.*

– 1 THESSALONIANS 5:18 (NLT)

Holiday birthdays can be confusing. My oldest daughter's birthday is near Thanksgiving, and several years ago, it fell right on Thanksgiving day. Because we didn't want her to feel ripped off, we did birthday stuff in the morning and ate Thanksgiving dinner with family in the afternoon.

It seemed like a good compromise. While she was sleeping, we decorated the house with princess banners and balloons. Then, we sneaked all of her presents out so we could start celebrating right after breakfast.

She loved it. We had birthday cake for brunch and spent the morning opening gifts and playing.

By the time the extended family arrived, however, we had shifted into full Thanksgiving mode. We served up the turkey and all the trimmings just as the Macy's parade was wrapping up. We'd planned the whole day to perfection. Or so I thought.

That night when I went to tuck my daughter into bed, I asked her, "Honey, did you have a fun Thanksgiving?" She paused, looked at me like I was crazy and said, "It was Thanksgiving?"

Okay, so maybe we didn't do such a great job of blending birthday and holiday celebrations. My daughter thought the elaborate feast and a house overflowing with family were just for her. The good people of New York City even threw her a big parade.

If we're honest, though, she's not the only one to miss the meaning of Thanksgiving. By the time we cook, eat, clean, watch football and cram in time with family, it can be easy to forget that Thanksgiving is a day set aside to give thanks for the blessings we all enjoy.

In some seasons it's easier to give thanks than others. Some years our circumstances make it difficult to see the positive in our lives. For most of us, though, we don't neglect Thanksgiving out of bitterness. We neglect it out of busyness. These days you can even get a jump on your holiday shopping before the turkey has grown cold.

I guess on my daughter's birthday I needed to stop and remind her that Thanksgiving is a big deal, not just the holiday, but the habit of expressing gratitude to a God who loves and cares for His kids. On most Thanksgivings I need someone to do the same for me.

It may sound corny to go around the table expressing what you're thankful for this year. It may feel even more awkward to offer a prayer of thanks to the God who is the giver of all good things. But true gratitude energizes our spirits by reminding us that the day isn't about us. No day is. We're the recipients of blessings and not the source.

However we celebrate the holiday this year, I hope none of us miss out. I hope there will be a point in the day when we just stop and realize that we are loved far more than we could ever deserve and our hearts will be overflowing with thanks.

126

NOTES

1. "Australian man sets new world record with highest-ever number of lights on Xmas tree," *News.com.au*, November 28, 2015, http://www.news.com.au/technology/innovation/design/australian-man-sets-new-world-record-with-highestever-number-of-lights-on-xmas-tree/news-story/80918e506f0e6c6adca47561a2072e9b.

2. Alysia Gray Painter, "'World's Tallest Live-Cut Tree' Arrives in LA," *NBCLosAngeles.com*, October 19, 2016, http://www.nbclosangeles.com/news/local/Worlds-Tallest-Live-Cut-Tree-Arrives-in-LA-397605391.html.

3. "Largest Christmas stocking: 1,600-Pound Stocking breaks Guinness World Records record," *WorldRecordAcademy.com*, December 13, 2015, http://www.worldrecordacademy.com/society/largest_Christmas_stocking_1600-Pound_stocking_breaks_Guinness_World_Records_record_215598.html.

4. David Sharp, "Giant 'snowman' stands tall," *SeacoastOnline.com*, March 1, 2008, http://www.seacoastonline.com/article/20080301/NEWS/803010319.

5. Clement Clarke Moore, *Twas the Night before Christmas*, 1823, accessed October 26, 2016, https://www.carols.org.uk/twas_the_night_before_christmas.htm.

6. Francis Thomson, *The Hound of Heaven*, 1893, accessed October 26, 2016, http://www.bartleby.com/236/239.html.

7. Dallas Willard, *Renovation of the Heart*. (Colorado Springs: NavPress, 2002), 14.

8. *Away In a Manger*, lyrics accessed October 25, 2016, http://www.hymnary.org/text/away_in_a_manger_no_crib_for_a_bed.

9. Lindsey Seavert, "Minnesota boy's Christmas gift returned by Utah trooper," *USA Today*, January 12, 2015, http://www.usatoday.com/story/news/nation/2015/01/12/minnesota-boy-gift-returned-utah-trooper/21621819/.